This book belongs to

....

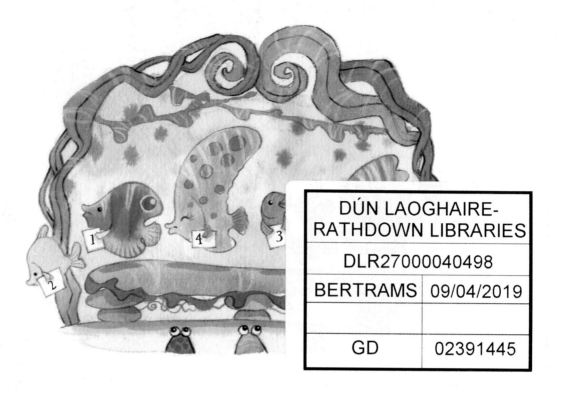

Quarto is the authority on a wide range of topics.

Quarto educates, entertains and enriches the lives of our readers—enthusiasts and lovers of hands-on living.

www.quartoknows.com

© 2019 Quarto Publishing plc

First published in 2019 by QED Publishing, an imprint of The Quarto Group.
The Old Brewery, 6 Blundell Street,
London N7 9BH, United Kingdom.
T (0)20 7700 6700 F (0)20 7700 8066
www.QuartoKnows.com

A catalogue record for this book is available from the British Library.

ISBN 978-1-78603-604-9

Based on the original story by Peter Bently and Daniel Howarth
Author of adapted text: Katie Woolley
Series Editor: Joyce Bentley
Series Designer: Sarah Peden

Manufactured in Dongguan, China TL112018

9 8 7 6 5 4 3 2 1

MIX
Paper from responsible sources
FSC® C104723
www.fsc.org

Reading
Gems

Top Spot

QED

Flat Fizz was off to the sea fair.
He wished he swam fast like Sprat.

There you are,
Fizz. Quick!

5

Fizz wished he was bright like Dot.

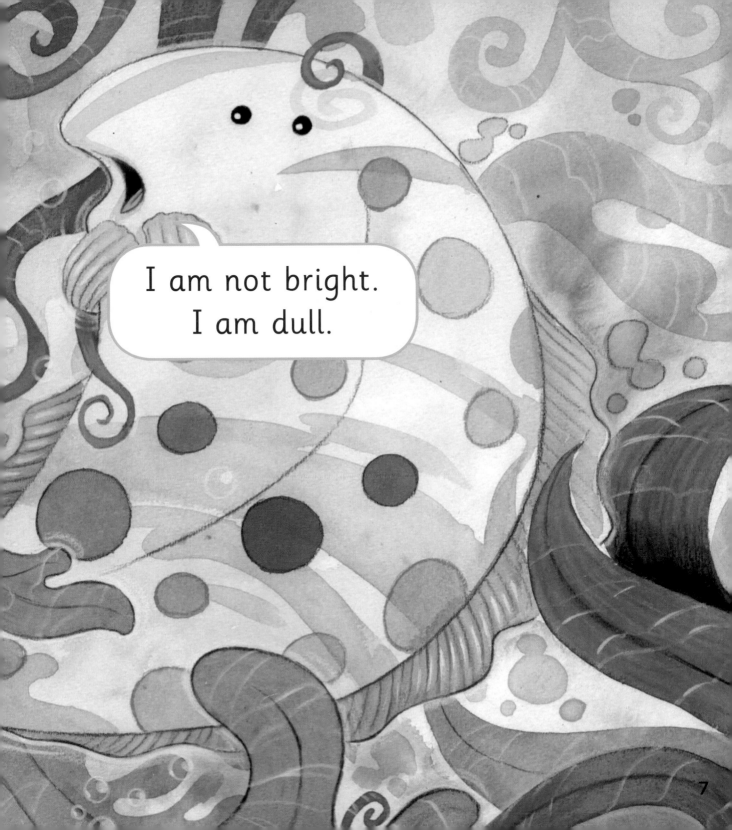

Puff liked to puff up very big.
Fizz wished he was funny like Puff.

All the friends had fun at the fair.

The fish went on ride after ride.

Sprat was quick!
He won the fast
fish race.

Dot got the top
spot for being
a bright fish.

Puff won a prize for being the best funny fish!

Flat Fizz was not fast or bright or funny.
He did not try out for the talent show.

I am slow and dull and flat.

Then Puff, Sprat and Dot
raced up to Fizz.

Shark wants
to eat us!

17

Where had all the fish gone?

They were under Flat Fizz!

I want to eat a fish!
Where are they?

Fizz was happy to help his friends.
He was the best at helping.

You hid us under you!

The fish were all happy.

Fizz was happy too...

He had won a prize! He got Top Spot for helping his friends!

Story Words

bright

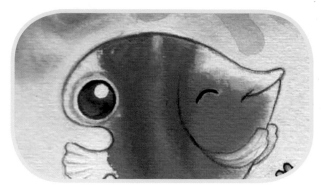

Dot

fast

Flat Fizz

funny

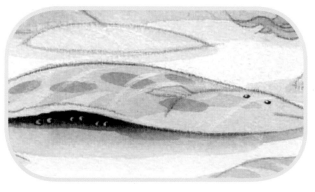

hid

prize

Puff

ride

shark

Sprat

talent show

25

Let's Talk About Top Spot

Look at the book cover.

Talk about the environment. What is the sea like?

What animals live in the sea?

What sounds might you hear at sea?

Why is Fizz sad at the beginning of the story?

What makes Fizz special?

Why is Fizz a good friend?

Why is he happy at the end of the story?

The story is set deep under the sea.

Have you ever been to the sea? What do you like about it?

Can you describe the sea? Think about how the sea feels, smells and tastes.

Draw a picture of some of the animals that live in the sea.

Can you draw one big sea creature and three little ones?

If you could be a sea animal, what would you choose to be? Why?

Did you like the story?

Who was your favourite character?

Fun and Games

Look at the pictures and read the words.
Which words have a 'sh' sound?

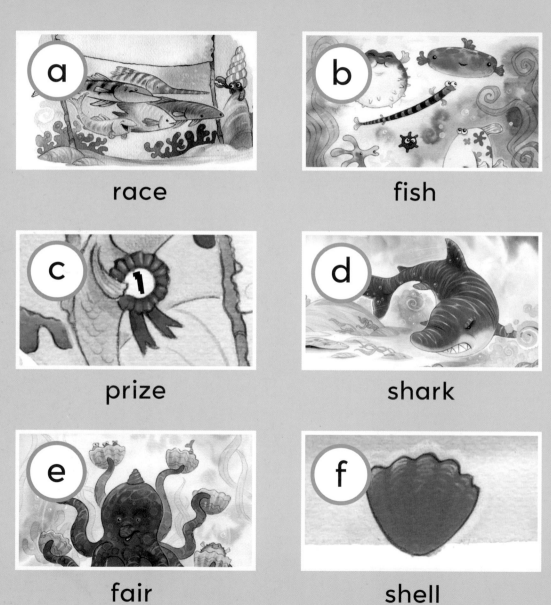

a race

b fish

c prize

d shark

e fair

f shell

Answer: b: fish; d: shark and f: shell all have the 'sh' sound.

Can you match these sentences to the correct character in the story?

I want to eat a fish!

Shark wants to eat us!

I am slow and dull and flat.

Roll up! Roll up!

Answers: Shark says, "I want to eat a fish!"; Fair worker says, "Roll up! Roll up!"; Flat Fizz says, "I am slow and dull and flat." and the friends say, "Shark wants to eat us!"

Your Turn

Now that you have read the story,
have a go at telling it in your own words.
Use the pictures below to help you.

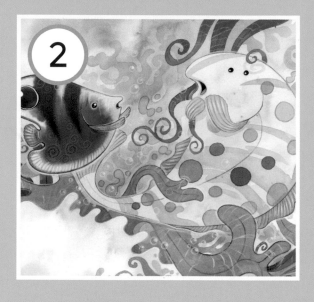

GET TO KNOW READING GEMS

Reading Gems is a series of books that has been written for children who are learning to read. The books have been created in consultation with a literacy specialist.

The books fit into five levels, with each level getting more challenging as a child's confidence and reading ability grows. The simple text and fun illustrations provide gradual, structured practice of reading. Most importantly, these books are good stories that are fun to read!

Phonics is for children who are learning their letters and sounds. Simple, engaging stories provide gentle phonics practice.

Level 1 is for children who are taking their first steps into reading. Story themes and subjects are familiar to young children, and there is lots of repetition to build reading confidence.

Level 2 is for children who have taken their first reading steps and are becoming readers. Story themes are still familiar but sentences are a bit longer, as children begin to tackle more challenging vocabulary.

Level 3 is for children who are developing as readers. Stories and subjects are varied, and more descriptive words are introduced.

Level 4 is for readers who are rapidly growing in reading confidence and independence. There is less repetition on the page, broader themes are explored and plot lines straddle multiple pages.

Top Spot is all about a fish who thinks he isn't as good as his friends. It explores themes of differences, friendship and sea creatures.